EDUCATION OBSERVED

SPECIAL NEEDS ISSUES

A SURVEY BY HMI

HER MAJESTY'S INSPECTORATE
LONDON: HMSO

CONTENTS

PREFACE

Since January 1983 the Secretary of State for Education and Science has published reports made available to him by Her Majesty's Inspectorate (HMI) following formal inspections of a range of educational institutions in England. Individual reports are followed up with local education authorities and/or with others responsible in each case by the Department of Education and Science (DES). HMI has also produced periodic reviews, incorporating information obtained through survey work and through individual visits as well as from published reports, under the title 'Education Observed'.

The present booklet uses as its starting point the findings and recommendations of the report of the Committee of Enquiry into the Education of Handicapped Children and Young People (the Warnock Committee), published in 1978. Within this framework, it draws on the recent work of HMI to present an outline of current dominant issues in the field of special educational needs in England and to review progress made over the past decade. On this basis, and taking account of current legislation and declared DES policies and guidance, it attempts to provide some estimate of the state of preparedness in this field for the likely challenges of the 1990s.

The booklet is addressed in the main to education officers, advisers, inspectors, governors and teachers. It will also be of interest to parents, doctors, nurses, social workers and in some instances to those who themselves have special educational needs.

SUMMARY

The Warnock Report (*Special Educational Needs*) provided clear indications of the strengths and weaknesses in this country's educational provision in the late 1970s for children and young people with special educational needs (SEN). The report recommended many changes, including some which have since been implemented through the Education Act 1981. Recent reports by HMI indicate that in the 1980s there were valuable developments, mostly along the lines advocated in the report, but that this sector is not well prepared to meet the challenges of the 1990s, such as those of the National Curriculum and local management of schools (LMS).

● In many areas of the country the most significant shortfalls, evident across the various aspects of special education considered, are in clear statements of policy, in the detailed planning of the deployment of personnel and resources, in positive approaches to the management of existing premises and curricula, and in the systematic evaluation of work undertaken. Implementation of policies requires further consideration in relation to LEAs, to individual schools and to classes within schools.

● There has been much progress at the pre-school level, notably through partnership arrangements between professionals and parents, but there is still a need for help for a higher proportion of young children with learning difficulties. At the post-school level there are now many more special courses in colleges of further education, but students with special needs could benefit from more places on mainstream courses.

● The more pressing needs at all levels are for enhanced expertise, both among those specialising in this field and among teachers generally. The potential for this exists to the extent that there is much goodwill but, if schools are to meet the requirements of the Education Reform Act 1988, more progress must be made, particularly in assessing pupils' capabilities in curriculum terms and in providing them with a balanced and broadly based curriculum.

● All initial teacher training (ITT) courses now carry some introduction to special needs issues for all students, and many provide opportunities for some to develop further skills and understanding in this area, but the majority have yet to permeate special needs aspects through all subjects taught. Recent attempts to achieve this permeation have potential but are difficult to work out effectively in practice. Thorough monitoring will be required to assess whether permeation can be made to succeed generally. For qualified teachers, there are now more short in-service (INSET) courses and part-time advanced courses concerned with special education, though this increase is to some extent at the expense of full-time courses. There are indications that training has become more relevant to classroom practice, but it has yet to catch up with increasing demands on teachers' knowledge and skills.

● Assessment procedures leading to written statements of children's special educational needs are complex and time-consuming, with considerable variation across LEAs in quality and use of statements, and with many statements lacking in specificity. Despite evident weaknesses in practice, there are many instances in which statements do succeed in safeguarding children's rights, securing appropriate resources and improving monitoring of progress. DES Circular 22/89* gives guidance, revised in the light both of developments since the 1981 Act and of the provisions in respect of the National Curriculum, on the procedures for making assessments and statements.

● The integration of disabled children into ordinary schools has proceeded gradually, but only occasionally is it accompanied by the careful planning, training and resourcing needed for success. Subject to these conditions, there is scope for further integration of at least some of the small minority of children with special needs still educated outside ordinary schools. Within-class support in ordinary schools is a promising development but it is difficult to establish effectively. There is some good practice, but it is not yet possible to assess whether this approach is transferable to the generality of schools.

● The smaller number of children now placed in special schools includes a higher proportion with severe and complex learning difficulties. While teacher–pupil relationships are generally good, schools often have difficulties in providing an appropriately balanced and broadly based curriculum for such pupils. Schooling for pupils with emotional and behavioural difficulties gives particular cause for concern. Although working links between special schools and ordinary schools have increased, only rarely have special schools become the centres of expertise envisaged in the Warnock Report.

*Circulars may be obtained from the DES.

● Advisory and support services have developed considerably, with a shift in support services away from direct teaching of individuals and small groups and towards the provision of advice, guidance and in-service training. This shift of expertise away from the classroom creates gaps which need to be filled through further within-school staff development. There are shifts among advisers towards more general advisory work on an area basis. Thus there is increasing pressure, as is the case in teacher training institutions and in schools, for subject specialists to extend their repertoires to include special education. Psychological services are now more firmly placed within the education system and are developing INSET for teachers to complement their casework. There is still, in many areas, scope for extension of their work to pre-school and particularly to post-school levels.

● Awareness of information technology has increased greatly among teachers, but real expertise is still confined to the few. There are now many examples of successful use of information technology with pupils with special needs, but use tends to be in particular areas of the curriculum only, notably in the development of spoken and written language. Information technology resources have become widespread in special schools, where teachers have often been able to increase them through fund-raising, but access to such resources is still often a problem for pupils with special needs in ordinary schools.

1 INTRODUCTION

1.   This review considers developments in SEN which have occurred in England since the publication of the Warnock Report in 1978 and the enactment of the Education Act 1981 (the 1981 Act). It is based on the work of HMI, mostly on surveys carried out between 1983 and 1989, partly on full inspections of individual institutions, and partly on discussion with LEA advisers and others concerned with special education.

2.   For children and adults with SEN to make full use of their abilities, they require help beyond that provided for pupils and students in general. Usually their limitations are intellectual and/or social, but sometimes their learning difficulties are either compounded or caused by hearing impairment, visual impairment or physical disability. In a few cases, intellectual difficulties are specific, affecting progress in some areas of the curriculum, such as acquisition of literacy, more than in others.

3.   The Warnock Report made 225 recommendations, 28 of these clustering into three areas of first priority: provision for children under five, provision for young people over 16, and teacher training. Other major areas of concern included assessment, special education in ordinary schools, special education in special schools, roles of parents, curriculum development, LEA advisory and allied professional services, health and social services, relationships across professions, voluntary organisations, and research.

4.   The Warnock Report shifted the emphasis from categorisation of handicaps to consideration of individual needs and recommended that services should be planned on the basis of one child in five requiring some form of special educational provision at some stage. The outcome of inspection work by HMI over the subsequent decade has supported this estimate.

5.   This review is not comprehensive. It focuses on those areas in which the Warnock Report identified the state of special educational needs across the country at the time and in which work by HMI provides evidence of subsequent progress. The following sections take up the selected issues in the order in which they were presented in the Warnock Report.

6.   The Warnock Report recommended greater recognition of parents as their children's main educators, extension of nursery education, extension of peripatetic teaching services and further provision of professional advice.

7.   By the early 1980s, as can be seen from the 1983 Department of Education and Science publication *Young Children with Special Educational Needs*, many nursery schools and nursery units attached to primary schools included children with special needs among their intake, and some of the more handicapped young children attended nursery classes in special schools. While materials and activities were generally appropriate, only in about a third of the ordinary schools did the teachers match activities to children's abilities; even in the special school classes, few of the children followed programmes designed specifically to meet their individual needs.

8.   During the 1980s one highly significant stimulus to development in teaching and support services for parents of young children with special needs was the spread of Portage projects. The Portage system originated in the United States. It involves professionals and parents working together, usually in the home, to assess the skills of the children concerned, then devising, implementing and evaluating precisely targeted teaching programmes. Published materials provide a structure for the work, parents are encouraged to carry out as much of the teaching as they can, and professional support services are developed on a geographical area basis.

9.   Portage projects now exist in almost all LEAs. Their growth has been helped in recent years by the existence of the National Portage Association and by the funding, through Education Support Grants (ESG), of some 93 projects. Over the period 1987 to 1989, 13 of these projects were surveyed by HMI and evaluated through direct observation, discussions with LEA personnel and attendance at conferences and other forms of INSET, some of which were run by the National Portage Association.[10*]

10.   The findings of the survey were generally encouraging; most of the work seen indicated that systematic and effective teaching and learning were taking place. Records compiled and opinions expressed by the parents, home visitors and the various professionals involved in the projects indicated that the majority of the children concerned had made accelerated progress.

*For references see p.33.

11.   Regular home visiting, involving parents of varying social and cultural backgrounds, was the strongest feature of the projects. Successful visits were characterised by warm relationships, mutual trust and respect, clear demonstration of teaching techniques, agreement on specific activities, joint setting of targets, appropriate praise for success, systematic record-keeping, and flexible use of the Portage model rather than slavish adherence to it. Nine of the 71 visits, judged to be unsuccessful, showed few of these characteristics.

12.   Weaker features of the projects included limited success in making use of voluntary helpers, reliance on short-term contracts and associated problems of recruitment, and, in some cases, lack of co-operation among members of different professions. Some medical staff expressed the belief that parents were being given unrealistically high hopes. Within their geographical areas, the projects involved only small proportions of the children who could potentially benefit from provision of this kind.

13. The Portage model provides just one of several existing means of helping parents and their young disabled children. The extent to which LEAs will support Portage work as an integral part of their provision, once ESG funding for this model ceases, is unclear. Nevertheless, comparison of current arrangements with those reported more than a decade ago in the Warnock Report indicates that appreciable gains have been achieved.

14.   The Warnock Report recommended more opportunities for education beyond the age of 16 for young people with special needs, both through supported attendance on ordinary courses and through special classes. Provision was advocated in schools, further education (FE) institutions and adult training centres, to be supplemented by careers guidance as appropriate.

15.   Evidence of developments over the period 1983 to 1988 has been gathered through inspections of provision for students with SEN in over 100 maintained colleges of FE. The findings of these inspections were published, in the 'Education Observed' series of HMI reviews, in February 1989.[1] Subsequent inspection and consultation indicate that the trends identified in this publication are continuing.

16.   Over the past few years there has been a considerable increase in provision for a broader range of learners with special needs, many of whom have previously attended special schools. This provision, however, still falls short of meeting the full range of special needs in this age group, notably those of young people with emotional and behavioural difficulties or with severe and multiple disability.

17.   Most of the students attend special courses. The evidence from the relatively few instances in which they attend mainstream courses is that more could do this, given appropriate support. Not all establishments have developed the college-wide co-ordination needed, together with appropriate liaison with careers services, schools and other key external agencies, for effective provision. Some constructive examples of mutually beneficial liaison between staff and parents were seen.

18.   There are still unmet needs for INSET, among college staff generally as well as among those specialising in working with these students. Under the LEA Training Grants Scheme (LEATGS), the National Priority Area (NPA) funding is significantly improving this situation, notably with regard to INSET for managers and for staff whose major college involvement consists of teaching students with SEN.

19.   There is evidence that curriculum design and use of appropriate teaching techniques are improving, but analysis of student need, to distinguish between students of different ability levels, requires more emphasis. So do assessment of students' learning and evaluation of courses.

20. The impact of the Education Reform Act 1988 and of the guidance contained in associated DES circulars is evident in that it is beginning to be reflected in the strategic planning of LEAs. Consideration is being given to performance indicators and weightings to support the wider range of students with special needs entering FE. A number of LEAs have recently created senior posts with responsibilities for SEN in FE, at officer/adviser and at college levels.

21. Overall, starting from the very low baseline of a decade ago, improvements have been significant, though standards vary. There are cases in which good liaison has been established among a range of providers with the aim of achieving continuity and progression for the students. Models of good practice exist in some colleges, but to establish the work formally, and to offer experience of good quality for all students, it is necessary for managers of FE to incorporate consideration of this work into their more general strategic planning, both at LEA and at college levels.

22.   The Warnock Report included recommendations that a special education element for all students should be included in all courses of ITT, and that wherever possible these courses should also offer options, thus enabling some to pursue their interest in this field in more depth.

23.   During the latter half of the 1980s, ITT courses across the country changed considerably as a result of the work of the Council for the Accreditation of Teacher Education (CATE), which implemented the criteria presented in DES Circular 3/84. The Circular's main effect was to increase the time devoted to subject study but it did include the requirements that students would come to identify and understand the more common learning difficulties. These requirements continue to feature in the revised criteria, which were introduced in DES Circular 24/89 and which came into force on 1 January 1990.

24.   Another factor influencing special needs aspects of ITT courses has been the Government's intention, as expressed in paragraph 147 of the 1985 White Paper 'Better Schools', to shift training for specialists in SEN from the initial to the in-service phase. Reference is made in the next section to some of the ensuing changes.

25.   During the 1980s CATE drew on inspections of all the ITT courses, findings of some half of these being summarised in a survey report published by DES in 1987.* By the mid-1980s the majority of ITT courses included in the survey had taken up the Warnock Report recommendations to the extent of providing some introduction to special needs issues for all students, with the emphasis on work in ordinary schools, though the time devoted to these issues varied widely. The best provision involved some contact with special needs work throughout the course, linking lectures and discussions with practical teaching and assessment work in schools. In about a quarter of the institutions, the work was unsatisfactory in that these links with practical work in schools were not developed.

26.   Most courses offered options, thus enabling some students to develop further skills and understanding in this area, and such options were generally helpful. In a few institutions, though, options were offered without the general framework of an

*Quality in schools: The initial training of teachers, HMSO, 1987.

introduction for all, so in these institutions many of the students missed out on SEN work altogether.

27.   The least satisfactory aspects of courses generally were their attempts to implement what is commonly referred to as a permeation approach. This approach was increasingly a feature of courses and was usually adopted alongside the other approaches already referred to. The intention was that consideration of special needs issues would permeate the whole of the course and, more specifically, that work within each subject specialism would take full account of pupils' special needs. Only a few subject specialists managed to do this successfully however; it was achieved more often in mathematics and in English than in other subjects, where in a number of institutions it hardly featured at all.

28.   Inspection of SEN in ITT has continued on a light monitoring basis. Findings of an exercise which took place over the academic year 1988–89 showed that by this time all the 22 institutions visited were at least making use of a permeation approach, and that most were also making use of the two major approaches recommended in the Warnock Report: introductory elements for all and more specialised options for some.[9]

29.   In general, there were indications of improvement in quality of work beyond that reported in 1987. Quality varied considerably, however, with good practice continuing to be less frequent in examples of the permeation approach than the other two. Features associated with successful permeation included policy documents indicating how permeation of special needs is to be monitored, the involvement of a special needs co-ordinator in the planning of subject teaching, and staff development to ensure that good practice in one subject area can influence practice in another. The few institutions relying entirely on the permeation approach rarely achieved good practice.

30.   Not surprisingly, good practice comes from a judicious blend of all three approaches and strong links between institution-based work and school experience. However, institutions have reduced the time devoted to special needs elements and options in order to increase the proportions of their courses devoted to subject study and thus meet the CATE criteria. This increases the need for permeative aspects to be effective.

31. Overall, indications are that over the decade 1980–89 there were useful developments in special needs aspects of ITT courses, generally following the line of the Warnock Committee recommendations, and that there are improvements in the quality of provision. The emergence of the permeation approach, though not specifically a Warnock Committee recommendation, is compatible with the Committee's thinking and can be regarded as an extension of it. By no means fully effective in existing courses generally, it deserves some priority for consideration and evaluation in institutions' development plans.

5 IN-SERVICE TRAINING FOR TEACHERS

32. The Warnock Report recommended that a variety of short INSET courses be taken by the majority of serving teachers, and that one-year full-time courses or their part-time equivalent be available to teachers with defined responsibility for children with SEN.

33. The Warnock Report recommendations concerning INSET stimulated a number of developments over the decade 1980–89, including the establishment of one-term full-time courses for teachers with designated responsibilities for SEN in ordinary schools. Further impetus has been provided in recent years through the operation of the LEATGS and, within this, the identification of NPAs.

34. These NPAs include support for specialist training in the teaching of the hearing impaired and the visually impaired, where there is a statutory requirement for teachers to gain additional specialist qualifications. There is also a NPA for training in the teaching of children with severe learning difficulties where, although there is no statutory requirement for a separate qualification, there is also a need for specialist training beyond the scope of initial training.

35. The existence of NPA funding has ensured a continuing supply of specialists in these areas. These areas of training are currently in the final stages of a planned transition, following the recommendations of the Advisory Committee on the Supply and Education of Teachers in 1984, from the initial to the in-service phase, thus ensuring that teachers undertaking this specialist training in future will already be qualified and experienced in work with ordinary pupils.

36. While this transition is desirable, the extent to which it is successful in practice remains to be seen. Also yet to be seen are the effects on quantity of training of the reduction in 1990 of NPA funding from the 70 per cent level to the 65 per cent level. The training of designated teachers of SEN in ordinary schools, the training of teachers of SEN in FE, and the training of educational psychologists are also NPAs and account for almost half the provision for SEN supported under the LEATGS.

37. Since the introduction of the LEATGS, HMI has continued to undertake some monitoring of the development of the specialist teacher training courses. This, coupled with consultation between HMI and teacher trainers and LEA advisers, encouraged the issue of guidance concerning specialist training at school level, through the DES Teacher Training Circular Letter 1/88. This and further monitoring

have helped ensure that satisfactory and in the main comparable course structures are emerging in these particular NPAs.

38.   LEATGS funding has led to a shift away from one-year full-time award-bearing courses to their part-time equivalents, often offered on a modular basis, and a considerable development in short courses managed by LEA advisers and by teachers themselves. Teacher trainers have generally structured their courses appropriately, and co-operation between LEA advisory services and training institutions has increased, but evaluation by LEAs of INSET available to their teachers has rarely been satisfactory.

39.   Over 1988–89 a particular focus of INSET for teachers concerned with SEN was preparation for the introduction of the National Curriculum. Within the mainstream of both the LEATGS and ESGs, substantial provision has been made for implementation of the National Curriculum generally. However, within the field of SEN, its extent has varied from one specialism to another. In the Midlands, for example, there has been a relatively high level of activity with respect to children with severe learning difficulties. Teacher trainers, teachers and advisers have together established working groups to develop programmes enabling these children to participate in the National Curriculum.

40.   While there have been INSET activities related to the National Curriculum in special schools across the country, at the end of the 1988–89 year few schools were in a position to provide the breadth of curriculum needed. In some instances, expertise in the subjects receiving insufficient attention would best be introduced through new appointments, but in many cases existing staff could have been helped, through INSET, to acquire this. Needs for staff development were noted particularly with respect to science, technology and modern foreign languages. In schools for pupils with emotional and behavioural disorders , HMI identified a perpetuation of curricula modelled on primary education into work with secondary aged pupils. Staff in schools for pupils with moderate learning difficulties had progressed less than had staff of other special schools.

41.   There is increasing consideration of the potential of open learning materials, through initiatives supported by the DES in the development of distance learning courses for teachers of the hearing impaired, of the visually impaired and of children with language disorders. Also, INSET developments in colleges of FE for staff at

higher managerial levels as well as for those with major teaching commitments in the field of SEN are significant.

42. Overall, there have been many INSET developments in accord with the recommendations of the Warnock Report. There is an increased variety of short courses on offer, and their relevance to serving teachers has increased, but the increase in number of courses on offer has not as yet been sufficient to enable the majority of serving teachers to avail themselves of them.

43. The availability of substantial award-bearing courses for those wishing to specialise in work with SEN has increased, partly because of the shift to part-time modular courses, often run outside school hours, at the expense of one-year full-time courses. Whether the marked reduction in full-time courses will ultimately be of significance to the development of the profession has yet to be seen, but it would seem unwise to allow them to disappear altogether.

44. The Warnock Report recommended substantial revision of existing statutory assessment and review procedures, calling for more thoroughly multi-professional assessment, with greater emphasis on the education required and with involvement of parents as partners.

45. These recommendations strongly influenced the form of the 1981 Education Act, which placed particular duties on LEAs with respect to assessment, and of the associated guidance provided in DES Circular 1/83 (since replaced by Circular 22/89). The major outcome was multi-professional assessment leading to the statements of special educational needs, specifying in each case the needs, the special educational provision through which they could appropriately be met, and the school within which such education should take place.

46. While many of the children defined by the Warnock Report as having SEN would have been assessed on a multi-disciplinary basis, only some one in ten of them became the subjects of statements. According to the Education, Science and Arts Committee's 1987 report on the implementation of the 1981 Education Act, approximately 1.5 per cent of the total school population of England were in special schools, children with statements comprised 1.7 per cent of the school population and about a quarter of children with statements were in ordinary schools.

47. Statement procedures in different regions of the country were studied by a University of London Institute of Education project, funded by the DES; findings were published in 1988.* LEAs were found to make some appropriate use of statement procedures, but the procedures themselves were often time-consuming, LEAs varied widely in the extent to which they used them, partnership between professionals and parents was hard to achieve, LEAs did not collaborate sufficiently with health and social services agencies, and the statements tended to lack specificity. Acting on these findings, staff of the project produced training materials designed to help overcome identified weaknesses and disseminated these across local agencies on a regional basis in 1989.

*Goacher, B., Evans, J., Welton, J. and Wedell, K., *Policy and provision for special educational needs*, Cassell, 1988.

48.   Similar findings emerged from a restricted survey, undertaken by HMI in 1989, of provision in ordinary schools for pupils of primary school age with statements.[11] The survey included 43 schools in 11 LEAs. Again there was evidence of considerable delay in completing the statement process in some areas, statements often lacked detail and gave little guidance on pupils' curricular needs, and the need for additional resources was rarely quantified. The quality of supporting advice was much better, and in some instances excellent.

49.   Records of annual review procedures indicated that these varied considerably. Some appeared perfunctory, whereas others achieved full multi-professional consultation, with structured agenda and minutes distributed to all participants. Even where practice was otherwise good, there were instances in which parental views were incorporated rather than presented in their own right. Parents' contributions varied widely, with some evidently very knowledgeable about their rights and responsibilities. Some schools provided in-service training for parents to ensure that they had essential information, were aware of procedures and had acquired skills needed to contribute to debate.

50.   Following consultation, the DES replaced Circular 1/83 by Circular 22/89, which gives guidance on the procedures for making assessments and statements under the 1981 Act in the light of developments since that Act and of the requirements of the Education Reform Act. For example, a child's statement is required to specify any necessary modifications to or exemptions from any part of the National Curriculum, and to indicate how, despite any such exceptions, a broad and balanced curriculum will be maintained.

51. Overall, the Warnock Report has exercised a profound influence on assessment of special needs over the past decade. While the assessment procedures developed have been found to have their problems in implementation, and still need in many areas to be considered within the context of whole LEA strategies for SEN, they constitute a definite advance on the procedures prevalent in the 1970s. Revisions for the 1990s will be needed to secure their relevance to continuing curriculum development.

52.   The Warnock Report, while endorsing the support for integration expressed in Section 10 of the Education Act 1976, and while acknowledging a shift across European and North American countries towards the education of handicapped children in ordinary schools, did not adopt a wholly integrationist stance. It supported some further degree of integration, subject to certain conditions: planned entry, involvement of governing body, a designated specialist teacher, a school-based resource centre, a limit to the school's proportion of pupils with special needs, and a planning framework provided by the LEA. It also recommended that existing special classes and units be attached to ordinary schools rather than to other kinds of establishment, such as child guidance centres.

53.   Among the one fifth of the school population designated in the Warnock Report as having special educational needs at some time, the vast majority (some 90 per cent) are, and always have been, educated in ordinary schools. Some impression of the current quality of the education of these pupils can be gained from the outcomes of a survey, undertaken by HMI from January 1988 to summer 1989, of provision for pupils in the 10/11 + and 11/12 + age groups in 55 primary schools and 42 secondary schools spread across 38 LEAs.[8] Altogether, 290 pupils were tracked, and their work in a total of 487 lessons was observed.

54.   In about half the lessons seen, both in primary and in secondary schools, the standard of work was judged to be satisfactory or better. Some of the work was of particularly good standard and was differentiated to match well with individual pupils' needs, using a range of suitable methodology and often involving subject or class teacher in collaborative planning with a specialist teacher for SEN.

55.   In some of the schools, a major recent change had been the development of whole school policies for SEN, involving all the teachers in considering and working with pupils with SEN, rather than just leaving this to a minority of teachers, and including the parents of children with SEN in discussions about their children's education.

56.   In most of the schools, children with SEN were taken out of mainstream class groups and into small specialist teaching groups for part of each week. Almost half the primary schools and over one quarter of the secondary schools were providing additional teaching support for children with SEN in mainstream class groups for short periods of time each week.

57.   Most schools designated a teacher to be responsible for the co-ordination and development of work with children with SEN. Most of these designated teachers were experienced as teachers but had received only very short periods of specialist training for this work. In the primary schools most of those designated were also class teachers and had insufficient time allowed to enable them to fulfil their consultancy roles.

58.   Teaching children with SEN generally was accorded a high priority and was often a focus for review and development work in primary and secondary schools. However, despite these positive developments around half the work undertaken by pupils with SEN was still of less than satisfactory standard, and too many pupils still followed a curriculum with serious limitations in breadth, balance, differentiation, continuity and progression. It is clear that some primary and secondary schools will need to review their provision for pupils with SEN if they are to ensure that these pupils have full access to the National Curriculum.

59.   Over the past decade there have been significant moves in many areas towards retaining pupils with moderate learning difficulties in ordinary schools rather than placing them in special schools. These pupils have been helped through statement procedures, which ideally have identified the material resources and teaching support appropriate to pupils' education.

60.   The common weaknesses of statement procedures in practice have been outlined in the previous section. The extra resourcing for pupils with statements in ordinary schools is not always comparable with that available in special schools. Statement procedures, despite their limitations in practice, have also helped achieve an increased level of integration, in some geographical areas, of pupils with severe learning difficulties.

61.   The Education Reform Act requires that all pupils should have access to the National Curriculum, but the precise curriculum for pupils with statements of special educational needs under the 1981 Act can be prescribed in the statements themselves. The 1987 figures in the Education, Science and Arts Committee report indicate that at that time just under one in 200 children in ordinary schools in England were the subjects of statements under the Act, though there was and continues to be considerable variation from one LEA to another.

62.   Provision for children with statements in ordinary schools was sampled during 1989 through an exercise already mentioned, involving 43 schools catering for pupils within the primary age range in 11 LEAs. Inspection focused on three groups of pupils: those with severe learning difficulties, those with hearing or visual impairment, and those with speech and language disorders.

63.   In the 118 lessons observed the pupils worked mainly in ordinary classes, though in a few instances they were to be found outside the ordinary class setting, taught individually or in groups. Quality of provision varied considerably. Some of it was extremely good, with pupils happy and confident, full and valued members of their classes, making good progress in their work.

64.   In three-quarters of the lessons observed, the work set was differentiated satisfactorily, with the levels of difficulty of the work set to match the pupils' abilities, whereas in the remainder differentiation was by outcome only. In some classes, the fact that a child had a statement of SEN was almost incidental, as the general classwork was carefully matched to children's abilities. In others, the pupils with statements struggled with presentations or tasks beyond their levels of comprehension or competence, deriving little benefit from them.

65.   In over a quarter of the lessons the teachers' expectations of their classes as a whole were too low or otherwise inappropriate, resulting in poor quality work or behaviour. In some classes pupils with statements were not expected to participate in assigned tasks and were left to their own devices. Specialist staff generally used effective techniques: helping pupils with hearing impairment to speak more clearly, for example, and helping those with severe learning difficulties to help themselves.

66.   Class teachers did little individual teaching, even when staffing ratios were good enough to facilitate this. Class teachers rarely made use of diagnostic assessment; this was almost invariably undertaken by specialist staff. Despite these evident shortcomings in technical skills, overall quality of relationships between teachers and pupils with statements was good. Few pupils with statements, however, had access to a sufficiently broad and balanced curriculum.

67.   Attempts to integrate pupils of secondary age from special schools into ordinary schools can be fraught with difficulties, judging from a survey by HMI of Technical, Vocational and Education Initiative work carried out across eight

secondary schools, eight special schools and five colleges offering special education in FE.[6] Problems included lack of understanding among secondary school staff of the social demands on the incoming pupils, and insensitivity on the part of the secondary schools' pupils. There was likely to be greater success when the pupils from the special schools were provided with special courses and mixed with the pupils on the roll of the host school for only part of their time.

68.   Physically disabled pupils form another group increasingly educated in ordinary schools rather than in special schools. Their provision was the subject of an inspection exercise, undertaken over the period 1986–88, involving 31 primary and secondary schools and 35 special schools, spread across a number of LEAs. In about a third of the ordinary schools visited, the physically disabled were based in special units, with varying degrees of integration in ordinary classes, and in the rest they were based in ordinary classes.

69.   The quality of education varied in all three settings and was on the average neither better nor worse in ordinary schools than in special schools. Generally the pupils received kindly attention rather than highly effective teaching, though there were some examples of good practice. Good practice in integrating physically disabled pupils into ordinary schools was likely to be in schools which already catered effectively for children's different ability levels. Satisfactory entry required, but only occasionally received, careful preparation within the receiving schools and, in many instances, INSET for the teachers and a phased introduction of the pupils.

70.   Integrated mainstream education offered physically disabled pupils the advantages of access to a wide curriculum in normal surroundings but also entailed some sacrifice of the advantages available through the concentration of specialist equipment and therapeutic resources in special schools.

71.   Mention has been made already of shifts in recent years towards helping children with special needs within mixed ability classes rather than by taking individuals or small groups outside their normal classrooms. A survey conducted by HMI during 1986–88 in 10 LEAs, supplemented by correspondence with a further six authorities, provided indications of the effectiveness and changing roles of the support services provided.[4]

72. A major finding of this survey of support services was that there were advantages to within-class support, particularly when its form was carefully discussed and agreed between class teachers and support teachers, but that there was little planning. Withdrawal teaching was by contrast often well structured but not linked with classwork and the gains were thus unlikely to extend to the classroom.

73. Developments overall have been cautiously integrationist, as advocated in the Warnock Report, but not necessarily planned or monitored with the kind of rigour the report advocated. The indications are that further integration could be advantageous, at least for some of that small minority of children with special needs still educated outside ordinary schools, but only if it is carefully planned, adequately resourced and backed by appropriate INSET. Within-class support is a development which goes beyond arrangements envisaged generally in the Warnock Report and which is worthy of further monitoring by LEAs.

74. The Warnock Report forecast a continuing but reduced need for special schooling. It recommended that LEA special schools should extend their functions, strengthening their links with ordinary schools, offering short-term provision, providing specialist expertise and acting as resource centres. It recommended that the standards of special schools outside LEA control be monitored by the DES, drawing on the expertise of HMI.

75. Within the LEA sector, policies favouring integration, coupled with demographic trends, have resulted in some reduction in the special school population. For example, annual school population returns to the DES indicate that the number of pupils on roll in all special schools in England and Wales dropped from 120,292 in January 1981 to 100,501 in January 1988. The trend was not consistent across the country or across types of special school; it was marked in the case of schools for pupils with moderate learning difficulties. There have been school closures and amalgamations, and the trend has been towards smaller schools with a higher concentration of children with more severe learning difficulties and multiple handicap. Contrary to the general trend, there were increases in provision designated for pupils with emotional and behavioural disorders.

76. The quality of provision giving the most cause for concern is that for pupils with emotional and behavioural disorders, as can be seen from a survey by HMI during 1983–88 of 76 LEA special schools and units for these pupils.[3] Many lacked the specialist facilities, staffing and organisation needed for delivery of a broad and balanced curriculum. These limitations reflected inadequacies in accommodation and resources, absence of staff expertise and insufficient INSET training rather than staffing shortages as such. Teacher–pupil relationships were generally good but the quality of work was often disappointing. There were enough examples of good practice to demonstrate the feasibility of providing effectively for these pupils in special schools and units, but it is also clear that the difficulties in achieving this are considerable.

77. While falling rolls in special schools have resulted in a number of closures and amalgamations, these solutions are not invariably either desirable or practicable. Inevitably there will be a continuing need for special schools, some of which are likely to be quite small. Because of this, one focus of inspection during 1988–89 was on small special schools, each with fewer than 50 on roll. A survey of 36 such schools in

28 LEAs sought to explore the margins of their viability, to assess quality of education and to identify strategies through which small special schools could ensure their effectiveness.[7] Most kinds of disability and almost all types of special school were represented.

78.   Standards achieved in classrooms in the survey were generally satisfactory and compared well with standards achieved in larger special schools. All the schools in the survey were seen to be viable in terms of quality of learning and teaching, and there was no indication that a particular number of pupils on roll could be regarded as a limit below which satisfactory provision could not be made. Often, where a particular area of one school's work was seen to be weak, strategies in other schools had alleviated similar difficulties.

79.   While 80 per cent of the lessons observed were satisfactory or better, including 16 per cent which were of very good quality, it was evident that provision of a balanced and broadly based curriculum was a major problem in small special schools. Science was identified as an area particularly in need of strengthening.

80.   There were encouraging examples of schools successfully overcoming their own curricular limitations through various strategies, such as drawing on outside expertise to help in curricular planning, using material facilities available in other schools, and establishing programmes of staff development to overcome weaknesses in particular subject areas. There is a need for these compensatory strategies to be costed, as a means of enabling their success to be fully evaluated.

81.   Inspection of the relatively small number of non-maintained special schools and of independent schools catering wholly or mainly for pupils with SEN has focused mainly on the latter, primarily in connection with approval by the Secretary of State under Section 13 of the 1981 Act. Indications are that standards vary widely, with a number of these independent schools on the margins of viability and with quality of education which, within a single school, can fluctuate markedly from one year to the next.

82. Consideration of outcomes of the full range of inspection of special schools has yielded some examples of schools that have become specialist teaching and advisory centres of the kind advocated in the Warnock Report: gradually integrating a number of their pupils into ordinary schools, providing continuing support for these and other pupils with SEN in local schools, and providing INSET for local teachers. This kind of progress, however, is not common. The more common picture is that of schools grappling uneasily with the problems of small unit size and an increasingly challenging clientele.

9 ADVISORY AND SUPPORT SERVICES

83. The Warnock Report referred to advisers, peripatetic teachers and home visiting teachers as often undertaking valuable work but as being employed in fragmented services, with the different elements only tenuously related. At that time, only about two in three LEAs had an adviser for special education. The report recommended that LEAs re-structure and supplement staffing in order to secure effective advice and support for teachers of SEN through unified special education services.

84. The report saw school psychological services as best remaining separate from, but complementary to, the special education services, with educational psychologists central to assessment, helping teachers particularly in dealing with emotional and behavioural problems, and contributing to INSET courses run by special education services. The report recommended that the psychological services function across the age range from pre-school to 19 and that target staffing ratios double, to one to 5,000.

85. The period to the end of 1989 was one of continuing change, and by this time there were very few LEAs without an adviser or inspector co-ordinating advisory services for SEN, though in some of the smaller authorities education officer and adviser roles were fulfilled by one person. In some LEAs, advisory services for SEN were seen as being relevant to the most able as well as to the least able pupils. In some LEAs the duties of inspectors and advisers were being re-organised and in others there were significant uncertainties as to future developments.

86. In recent organisational changes each adviser for SEN has usually taken on general advisory responsibilities for a cluster of primary, secondary and special schools across an area of the LEA, with advisers for other specialisms taking on equivalent general responsibilities, including those for special schools, in other geographical areas. In a few LEAs there has been a significant shift from advisory work to inspection.

87. The need for subject advisers to develop their expertise throughout the ability range, including SEN in their remit, is a longstanding one and is generally recognised as such. It has not necessarily been met through the increase in the number of advisers appointed specifically with a remit for SEN. With general advisory responsibilities moving on to a territorial basis, this need is becoming more pressing.

Clearly, current organisational changes have strong implications for staff development work within LEA advisory and inspection services as a whole.

88.   Reference has already been made, in section 7 on special education in ordinary schools, to some of the findings of the 1986–88 survey of LEA support services. Within the LEAs considered, while these services were by no means fully co-ordinated, it was evident that they were less fragmented than had generally been the case when information was being gathered by the Warnock Committee. Some were well along the road to the unification recommended in the committee's report.

89.   Although there had undoubtedly been a number of developments, only a few of the 16 LEAs considered in the 1986–88 survey of support services had policy documentation setting out their work. Few of the services had clear lines of management and general recognition of the roles of staff in relation to those of staff of other advisory services within the same LEAs. Consequently, in too many cases staff of schools reported confusion concerning the practices of different services, and evidence was found of pupils receiving unco-ordinated assistance from a number of sources.

90.   Support services differed considerably from one LEA to another in the number and age ranges of pupils helped. Some focused only on pupils without statements, those with statements being helped by other means, and most concentrated on pupils of primary school age. Staff of services offered at both primary and secondary levels argued convincingly for these arrangements, pointing out the value of helping pupils to bridge from one to the other.

91.   In some LEAs, staff sought to monitor their work by measuring pupils' progress and seeking teachers' and parents' appraisals of the teaching, advice and INSET provided, but systematic approaches to evaluation of support services as a whole were not widespread.

92.   Staff of the most effective support services, as well as having their own roles clearly co-ordinated, worked in partnership with the heads, designated co-ordinators and class teachers in the schools concerned, carefully discussing the help they might offer and ensuring that any advice took realistic account of teachers' capabilities. Only in a few cases was there adequate time allowed on teachers'

timetables for the liaison and INSET needed to ensure that individual pupils' needs could be met.

93.   The survey identified changing roles among the advisory teachers employed in the support services, whereby the proportion of their time spent advising as opposed to teaching was increasing. This shift involved an increasing need for clerical time: in providing written programmes of work for individual pupils, for example, in corresponding with parents, and in preparing materials for use in INSET work with teachers. None of the services visited was thought by HMI to have sufficient clerical help to fulfil these roles.

94.   Some indication of recent developments in the work of educational psychologists was obtained through a survey, undertaken by HMI during 1988 and 1989, of LEA psychological services.[12]

95.   No attempt was made to quantify staffing nationwide for the purposes of this survey, but it was clear that across the LEAs visited there had been considerable increase in staffing over the past decade. It was also evident that there had been moves of location, often from accommodation rather peripheral to other aspects of education (for example, from child guidance clinics) into premises more central to it. While overcrowding was a common outcome of these two trends, shifts towards the centre clearly enhanced communication within the educational system.

96.   The organisational location of psychological services was also likely to be more clearly within education. It varied, though, and was not always in accord with the Warnock Committee recommendation that psychological services be separate from, but complementary to, special education services.

97.   Some principal educational psychologists were set within the special education division, some were responsible to the principal adviser and a few directly to the chief education officer. While location within the structure undoubtedly affected the principal psychologist's influence, the range of activities undertaken and the ways in which the service as a whole was perceived, it did not appear to be related to the quality of the work of the educational psychologists employed within it.

98.   Psychologists located within special education were more likely to be seen generally as being largely or exclusively concerned with pupils with SEN. Those within the principal adviser's sector generally carried a wider brief, were more

closely involved in central issues, and were more likely to be regarded as effective by officers of the LEA.

99.   Few psychological services had produced written policy documents, setting out their aims, objectives and range of activities, though staff in several had compiled procedural papers of use to parents as well as to professionals. Most of the principal psychologists adopted positive management strategies, though few drew on management training facilities existing within their LEAs, and some approaches were inappropriately laissez-faire.

100.   In appraising the quality of the work undertaken by educational psychologists, HMI observed them in action and discussed the work with the psychologists themselves and with their clients (mainly teachers). Most of the work seen took the form of assessment. The quality of assessment work was mainly good in itself, with some of it particularly perceptive and sensitive. In some instances, though, the work did not require psychological expertise and would have been more suitably handled by special education support service staff or by the schools themselves.

101.   While their ranges of activity varied considerably, the psychologists typically reported spending about 60 per cent of their time on individual assessment, treatment and associated writing, 20 per cent on administration and travel, and 20 per cent on INSET and allied advisory activities.

102.   Given psychologists' particular expertise and the needs of the education services generally, this allocation of time seemed broadly appropriate, though more selectivity in taking on referrals could have enabled them to devote more time to INSET activities designed to help teachers help themselves. Total time spent on INSET activities did appear to be increasing in a number of LEAs and there were several instances of new training posts having been funded through the LEATGS.

103.   Survey findings generally did not bear out the view, often expressed by psychologists, that implementation of the 1981 Act had unduly influenced their ways of working. It was the case, though, that in a few LEAs their work was dominated by formal assessment, taking up to 80 per cent of their time, of children referred as requiring statements of SEN. These instances, the result of a lack of effective procedures for completing statements, tended to be characterised by low morale and long delays.

104. Whether or not assessment of pupils' special needs was over-emphasised, this, together with ensuing recommendations, could easily prove to be contentious. From the psychologist's point of view there were often tensions between acting as advocate for a client and carrying out LEA policy. From the education officer's point of view there could be the decision as to whether to uphold publicly expressed opinions and thereby unduly strain existing resources.

105. Most psychologists were deployed on an area basis, each relating mainly to a cluster of primary schools and the secondary schools into which they fed. Alongside these general responsibilities, staff in most services were encouraged to develop special interests, though there were few specialist posts as such.

106. These arrangements appeared generally suitable to the tasks undertaken, particularly as they facilitated contacts with education officers and others taking responsibilities across the same geographical areas. The most noticeable weakness in deployment was that it was usually across a curtailed age range, with the focus on pupils of primary age. As a result, pre-school children were relatively neglected and students over the age of 16 particularly so.

107. Overall, the many developments in LEA advisory and support services have been largely, but not entirely, in the direction of the unification advocated by the Warnock Committee. The development of key working partnerships between advisory teachers, heads and teachers is achieved in some instances only. Further organisational changes appear likely, as advisory teachers shift from teaching to advisory roles and as specialist advisers move to more generalist advisory and inspectorial roles, often on an area basis. Developments in the roles of educational psychologists have placed them more firmly within the educational system and the amount of INSET they conduct has increased, but they still tend to work with children within a restricted age range.

108. Information technology was not a focus of consideration for the Warnock Report. Since the report's publication, however, innovation in information technology has developed dramatically, carrying many implications for the education of children with special needs. Government funding has assisted developments within special needs considerably, notably through the development of the four regional Special Education Microelectronics Resource Centres from 1982 to 1989, the two Aids to Communication in Education centres from 1984 and the Special Needs Software Centre from 1985.

109. Developments over the period 1983-89 were monitored through an exercise involving some 200 inspection visits by HMI specialising in uses of information technology with pupils and students with special needs, through supplementary visits carried out primarily for other purposes, through visits to resource centres concerned with information technology for SEN, through discussions with LEA advisers and officers, and through observation of INSET sessions.

110. Awareness of information technology has increased greatly among teachers, INSET at an introductory level has been extensive and there are now numerous examples of successful use of information technology with pupils and students with learning difficulties and/or physical disability and/or visual impairment. There have been notable developments in the use of speech synthesisers, braillers and alternative keyboards. Levels of awareness of the use of information technology to support those with SEN are not yet high among LEA advisers generally, and not even among advisers specialising in SEN.

111. Information technology equipment and software are present in almost all special schools, but as yet few staff have participated in INSET in sufficient depth to enable them to realise the full potential of available resources. Information technology is less prevalent in primary schools, and pupils with SEN tend to have particularly limited access to it. In secondary schools, use with pupils with SEN tends to be by specialists in SEN only, principally for consolidating skills rather than for more creative activities, and there is little awareness among subject specialists of the possibilities of information technology for these pupils.

112. While most schools and colleges now have a teacher who has responsibility for information technology resources, the fact that real expertise is still the province of the few means that there can be serious problems in schools when key staff leave.

The best practice in the support of pupils and students with SEN through information technology is associated with the use of a small number of powerful and flexible programmes. Such software can be used to teach pupils of all ages with many different special needs across the curriculum, but its successful introduction is dependent on effective INSET.

113. At present information technology tends to be used with pupils with SEN in limited areas of the curriculum only, notably in the development of spoken and written language, the latter through wordprocessing programmes in particular, and to a significant extent in mathematics. Some uses have been seen in personal and social development sessions. Science stands out as an area of the curriculum in which the potential of information technology remains largely unrealised.

114. The extensive educational legislation and guidance introduced during the late 1980s, notably through the Education Reform Act 1988 and associated Regulations, will inevitably lead to profound changes in the working of schools and colleges during the first half of the 1990s. While the framework for these changes is already largely in place, their detailed nature is difficult to forecast.

115. From the point of view of educational planners concerned with special educational needs, several elements of the Education Reform Act 1988 are highly significant. The Act includes the requirement that every pupil of school age has access to a balanced and broadly based curriculum, promoting personal development and preparing that pupil for adult life.

116. Within this framework there is the possibility, under sections 4 and 17 to 19 of the Act, that in any subject of the National Curriculum some pupils can be offered modified programmes of study or can be exempted from them. Similarly, these exceptional arrangements can occur with respect to attainment targets and procedures for assessment. The consensus emerging from the published reports of the subject working groups, strongly endorsed by the National Curriculum Council's special needs document, A Curriculum for All, published in October 1989, is that there will be few instances in which they will be needed.

117. As yet, policy has not been settled on the form in which schools' statutory assessment statistics should be published. There are issues to be resolved in that context about data on pupils with special needs. It would be consistent with the general approach to their participation in the National Curriculum for their results to be included within schools' overall figuring, but schools will want reassurance that this will not tell against them in any way. Measures which show pupils' progression from different starting points may be one answer.

118. The Education Reform Act 1988 allows for the establishment, as described in DES Circulars 10/88 and 21/89, of a new class of maintained schools called grant-maintained schools. By May 1990 29 grant-maintained schools had been established. They will continue to have the same obligations as regards provision for pupils with special educational needs as do all other maintained schools and they will continue to be able to call on the services of the educational psychologists of their former maintaining LEAs. They will also equally be open to HMI inspection and monitoring on the same basis as applies to LEA maintained schools.

119. The scheme for LMS, as presented in DES Circular 7/88, includes consideration of the education of pupils with special needs in ordinary schools. One key consideration is the way in which each LEA's formula for allocation of resources takes account of special needs. LMS does not at present apply to special schools and will not do so unless and until the Secretary of State makes Regulations bringing them within its compass.

120. Implementation of the Children Act 1989 will place new duties on independent residential schools, with respect to the welfare of pupils. It will call for increasing involvement of the staff of the Social Services Inspectorate and local authority Social Services Departments in monitoring the schools' welfare arrangements.

121. Issues referred to so far in this section illustrate various possibilities with regard to future changes in educational practice. There are others, for example those relating to teacher supply, levels of educational funding and the contributions of information technology. Given these possibilities, how well prepared is existing provision for special educational needs to meet the challenges of the 1990s? While there have been many valuable developments during the decade since the publication of the Warnock Report, the state of preparedness overall is not great. In the remaining paragraphs, matters in particular need of attention are identified in broadly the order to which they have been referred in the main text.

122. Provision for pre-school children and that for students beyond the age of 16 continue to be of high priority within the field of special needs. Within these groups, educational provision found to be of merit could usefully be extended to benefit all those seeking access to it. Learning programmes available to both groups need to be looked at from the standpoint of the National Curriculum, as modified in the schools concerned, to ensure continuity from one phase of education to another. Continuity will also be enhanced if staff concerned with early and late stages of schooling monitor their own provision from this perspective.

123. Within ITT the need is not so much for extra provision as for more effective application of permeation techniques already being introduced with only occasional success. As pupils varying widely in ability are introduced to the National Curriculum, it becomes imperative that tutors specialising in the

teaching of particular subjects are able to help their students identify and implement programmes of study suitable for pupils who, while being taught within a particular age group, are functioning at levels different from that of the majority.

124. Once trainees have developed sufficient competence to qualify as teachers, they will require continuing training on an in-service basis and their need to develop skills in curriculum-based diagnostic assessment may well deserve priority. Information technology, with a potential as yet barely even touched on in most areas of the curriculum, must emerge as another area of priority for in-service training.

125. When children are assessed under the Education Act 1981, the curriculum recommended for them must be balanced and broadly based, and any modifications to or exemptions from the National Curriculum must be specified. While educational psychologists are likely to remain central to the assessment process, assessment will clearly need to be curriculum-based, and expertise across the curriculum will be required. Development and application of this expertise will be enhanced if psychologists work in close collaboration with advisers and inspectors carrying subject specialisms as well as with those concerned with special needs.

126. While there is scope for further integration of pupils with special needs within ordinary schools, this needs to be undertaken with great care, particularly with respect to curriculum breadth and balance. Within-class support for pupils with special needs can be of value but this is difficult to implement effectively. In monitoring the effectiveness of integration and within-class support, LEAs will need to take full account of costs as well as of benefits. LEAs, governors, teachers and parents are likely to be faced with difficult tasks in ensuring that these pupils' rights are sustained.

127. Consideration of staffing levels appropriate to pupils with special educational needs, whether they are in ordinary schools or special schools, should be informed by the guidance in the draft DES Circular 'Staffing for pupils with special educational needs', issued in January 1990.

128. Staff of special schools, irrespective of whether they participate in LMS schemes, are presented with particular difficulties in making the changes necessary to meeting the requirements of the Education Reform Act. Initially there is the undertaking of revising their pupils' existing statements of special educational needs, ensuring that the curriculum prescribed for each pupil is balanced and broadly based, and specifying any departures from the National Curriculum. This should at least serve to identify schools' deficiencies with respect to staffing expertise, resources and curriculum on offer. Then there will be the task of planning the allocation of available resources to make good any deficiencies found. Indications of recent inspection are that science is an area in particular need of strengthening.

129. In monitoring their own implementation of the Education Reform Act, LEAs may increasingly call on staff of their advisory services concerned with special needs to take on more general inspection roles, with support services carrying out advisory rather than teaching functions. With the management of schools devolved to the schools themselves, governors and heads will have more direct responsibilities for arrangements through which they secure and develop the teaching expertise they require. Under these arrangements, within-school consultants, external advisers, psychologists and others providing advice and training may become increasingly accountable to the schools, having to convince governors and heads that their services offer value for money.

130. This review has drawn on a range of inspection exercises undertaken by HMI over the period 1983–89; each of these exercises was reported in its own right during 1989–90. The following have already been published and copies are available, free of charge, from Department of Education and Science Publications Despatch Centre, Honeypot Lane, Stanmore, Middlesex HA7 1AZ.

Publications

1. *Education Observed 9: Students with Special Needs in Further Education,* 1989.

2. *Education Observed 11: Hospital and Home Education Services,* 1990.

Reports

3. *A Survey of Provision for Pupils with Emotional/Behavioural Difficulties in Maintained Special Schools and Units* (62/89).

4. *A Survey of Support Services for Special Educational Needs* (75/89).

5. *Educating Physically Disabled Pupils* (110/89).

6. *Special Education within TVEI* (116/89).

7. *Effectiveness of Small Special Schools* (279/89).

8. *A Survey of Pupils with Special Needs in Ordinary Schools* (337/89).

9. *Special Educational Needs in Initial Teacher Training* (18/90).

10. *Portage Projects: A Survey of 13 Projects Funded by Education Support Grants* (25/90).

11. *Primary Aged Pupils with Statements of Special Educational Needs in Mainstream Schools* (40/90).

12. *Educational Psychology Services in England* (119/90).

The following publication is in preparation:

Education Observed: Information Technology and Special Educational Needs in Schools (HMSO).

Education Observed series

Education Observed: A review of the first six months of published reports by HM Inspectors, 1984

Education Observed 2: A review of HMI reports on primary schools and 11–16 and 12–16 comprehensive schools, 1984

Education Observed 3: Good teachers, 1985

Education Observed 4: Homework, 1987. Out of print.

Education Observed 5: Good behaviour and discipline in schools, 1990

Education Observed 6: Effective youth work, 1987

Education Observed 7: Initial teacher training in universities in England, Wales and Northern Ireland, 1988

Education Observed 8: Learning assignments in vocational further education, 1990

Education Observed 9: Students with special needs in further education, 1989

Education Observed 10: Curriculum continuity at 11-plus, 1990

Education Observed 11: Hospital and home education services, 1990

Education Observed 12: The Lower-Attaining Pupils' Programme 1982–88, 1990

Education Observed 13: Attendance at school, 1990

Education Observed 14: Girls learning mathematics, 1990

To obtain these free publications contact:
Department of Education and Science
Publications Despatch Centre
Honeypot Lane
Stanmore
Middx HA7 1AZ
Tel: 081-952 2366

Two fully illustrated publications linked to this series are:
'Our policeman': Good practice in police/school liaison, 1989.
Free (available as above)
Better Libraries: Good practice in schools, HMSO, 1989. £2.95

Printed in the United Kingdom for HMSO
Dd 292431 C60 6/90